HALEY MᶜGEE

Haley McGee is an actor, writer and theatremaker. Born and raised in Kitchener-Waterloo, Canada, at seventeen she moved to Toronto where she received a BFA in acting from the Toronto Metropolitan University and subsequently worked there as an actor and playwright until she relocated to London in 2016.

In addition to *Age is a Feeling*, Haley has created four other solo shows, including sold-out hit *The Ex-Boyfriend Yard Sale*, which has also been adapted into a full-length book, published by Hodder and Stoughton in 2021. Her award-winning solos have toured to thirty-seven venues in eleven countries and been translated into four languages.

Haley also teaches artists how to create their own solo shows and self-produce their own theatre projects.

www.haleymcgee.ca

Other Titles in This Series

Annie Baker
THE ANTIPODES
THE FLICK
JOHN

Lily Bevan
ZOO & TWELVE COMIC MONOLOGUES FOR WOMEN

Jez Butterworth
THE FERRYMAN
JERUSALEM
JEZ BUTTERWORTH PLAYS: ONE
JEZ BUTTERWORTH PLAYS: TWO
MOJO
THE NIGHT HERON
PARLOUR SONG
THE RIVER
THE WINTERLING

Jessie Cave
SUNRISE

Caryl Churchill
BLUE HEART
CHURCHILL PLAYS: THREE
CHURCHILL PLAYS: FOUR
CHURCHILL PLAYS: FIVE
CHURCHILL: SHORTS
CLOUD NINE
DING DONG THE WICKED
A DREAM PLAY *after* Strindberg
DRUNK ENOUGH TO SAY I LOVE YOU?
ESCAPED ALONE
FAR AWAY
GLASS. KILL. BLUEBEARD'S FRIENDS. IMP.
HERE WE GO
HOTEL
ICECREAM
LIGHT SHINING IN BUCKINGHAMSHIRE
LOVE AND INFORMATION
MAD FOREST
A NUMBER
PIGS AND DOGS
SEVEN JEWISH CHILDREN
THE SKRIKER
THIS IS A CHAIR
THYESTES *after* Seneca
TRAPS
WHAT IF IF ONLY

Phoebe Eclair-Powell
DORAIN *with* Owen Horsley
EPIC LOVE AND POP SONGS
FURY
HARM
WINK

Sophie Ellerby
LIT

Natasha Gordon
NINE NIGHT

Rose Heiney
ELEPHANTS
ORIGINAL DEATH RABBIT

Tatty Hennessy
A HUNDRED WORDS FOR SNOW
SOMETHING AWFUL

Anna Jordan
CLOSER TO GOD
CHICKEN SHOP
FREAK
POP MUSIC
THE UNRETURNING
WE ANCHOR IN HOPE
YEN

Arinzé Kene
GOD'S PROPERTY
GOOD DOG
LITTLE BABY JESUS & ESTATE WALLS
MISTY

Nicôle Lecky
SUPERHOE

Laura Lomas
BIRD & OTHER MONOLOGUES FOR YOUNG WOMEN
CHAOS

Benedict Lombe
LAVA

Cordelia Lynn
HEDDA TESMAN *after* Ibsen
LELA & CO.
LOVE AND OTHER ACTS OF VIOLENCE
ONE FOR SORROW
THREE SISTERS *after* Chekhov

Rob Madge
MY SON'S A QUEER (BUT WHAT CAN YOU DO?)

Suzie Miller
PRIMA FACIE

Margaret Perry
COLLAPSIBLE

Winsome Pinnock
LEAVE TAKING
ROCKETS AND BLUE LIGHTS
TAKEN
TITUBA

Lauryn Redding
BLOODY ELLE

Stef Smith
ENOUGH
GIRL IN THE MACHINE
HUMAN ANIMALS
NORA : A DOLL'S HOUSE
REMOTE
SWALLOW

Ciara Elizabeth Smyth
SAUCE & ALL HONEY

Izzy Tennyson
GROTTY & BRUTE

debbie tucker green
BORN BAD
DEBBIE TUCKER GREEN PLAYS: ONE
DIRTY BUTTERFLY
EAR FOR EYE
HANG
NUT
A PROFOUNDLY AFFECTIONATE, PASSIONATE
  DEVOTION TO SOMEONE (–NOUN)
RANDOM
STONING MARY
TRADE & GENERATIONS
TRUTH AND RECONCILIATION

Various
15 HEROINES: 15 MONOLOGUES ADAPTED FROM OVID
HERETIC VOICES
THE MOTHERHOOD PROJECT
SNATCHES: MOMENTS FROM 100 YEARS OF
  WOMEN'S LIVES

Phoebe Waller-Bridge
FLEABAG

Martha Watson Allpress
PATRICIA GETS READY (FOR A DATE WITH THE MAN
  THAT USED TO HIT HER)

Camilla Whitehill
MR INCREDIBLE

Age is a Feeling

HALEY McGEE

NICK HERN BOOKS

London

www.nickhernbooks.co.uk

A Nick Hern Book

Age is a Feeling first published in Great Britain as a paperback original in 2022 by Nick Hern Books Limited, The Glasshouse, 49a Goldhawk Road, London W12 8QP

Reprinted with revisions in 2022

Age is a Feeling copyright © 2022 Haley McGee

Illustrations copyright © Jason Logan

Haley McGee has asserted her right to be identified as the author of this work

Designed and typeset by Nick Hern Books, London
Printed in Great Britain by Mimeo Ltd, Huntingdon, Cambridgeshire PE29 6XX

A CIP catalogue record for this book is available from the British Library

ISBN 978 1 83904 116 7

Age is a Feeling was first performed at Soho Theatre, London, on 27 July 2022. It played at Summerhall as part of the Edinburgh Festival Fringe from 3–28 August 2022, before transferring back to Soho Theatre on 6 September 2022 for a three-week run, returning for a four-week run from February 2023. The creative team was as follows:

Writer and Performer	Haley McGee
Director and Dramaturg	Adam Brace
Scenic Designer	Zoë Hurwitz
Lighting Designer	Daniel Carter-Brennan
Stage Manager	Rose Hockaday
Producer	David Luff and Maddie Wilson for Soho Theatre
PR	Chloé Nelkin Consulting

Short excerpts and work-in-progress performances of *Age is a Feeling* took place at Camden People's Theatre, the Rosemary Branch Theatre, Soulpepper Theatre's Fresh Ink series, Brainchild's Hatch and Soho Theatre. It was commissioned by Soho Theatre.

No one gets to know everything about your life
Not even you
Here are twelve stories about what's to come in your adult years
Starting when you're 25, and going...
And today, you'll choose which stories you'll hear and which you won't
You'll choose the first two now

Good
That's decided

Happy 25th birthday
In anticipation of your celebration
These flowers were collected from the cemetery
Along with this message for you:

Age is a feeling
You'll feel it
When you turn 25
(And realise that one day you will die)
The feeling begins as fear

Do you know why? your father will ask, placing both his palms down on the table. Why they won't let you rent a car until you turn 25?
You'll shake your head, mouth filled with slightly dry chocolate cake. Mm mmn.

Because your brain isn't done developing until now.

You'll be celebrating this birthday in your childhood home,
with your parents and brother
And you won't know it now, but you'll never do this again

It takes about twenty-five years for your thinking to move
from your amygdala to your prefrontal cortex.
Your mother gives you the eyebrows, He heard this on the
radio.

So! 25 is the real beginning of adult life.
Beginning!? I was a parent, with a mortgage, by the time I was
25!
Alright, Mom. Your generation had it all figured out and
we're... Your older brother grins at you. We're good for
nothing.
Oh no! You're good for everything! Your mom will say, sliding
her wine glass out of her own reach.
And you'll reply, Mom. It's fine. I'm your favourite
disappointment. Just give me time.

But a persistent sense that time is accelerating and you are
not keeping up will burrow into your psyche
And next thing, you'll be consumed
With fear
Fear of your time running out
Fear of your life being ripped from you, too soon:
In a car crash
Drowning in the bath
Crushed by a falling piece of concrete on a Tuesday afternoon

You'll fear dying from a disease—
Then be grateful when it's *not* the thing you convinced
yourself it was
Leaving the doctor's surgery, you'll truly understand

Your health *is* everything
But you'll be back to drinking too much and sleeping too little
in no time, because life is short and fuck it, you'll sleep when
you're dead

And you'll have ambitions to pursue but no clue how to tackle
them
You'll try to reassure yourself that age is a feeling
But you feel it
You're scared

You want to slow time down
Log every memory
Heed every lesson
Know everything
But you can't
You don't get to know everything
And no one gets to know everything about you, not even
yourself

At 26, in the wake of your first shattering heartbreak
(The one that teaches you that love *is* conditional)
You'll take solace at the dog park near your house
You've always wanted a dog—but someone close to you was
always allergic—and so in lieu of getting your own, watching
other people's dogs tussle and chase each other is good
medicine for your broken heart
And there, one day, sitting on the edge of the dog park

> An acquaintance of yours will pass by, spot you
> ogling dogs, and stop to say hi
> They'll introduce you to the stranger beside them,
> a woman in a trench coat with dark eyeliner and a
> scar on her cheek

OYSTER

TOGETHER YOU MAKE A PACT TO LIVE INTERESTING LIVES THAT DEFY CONVENTION

Which one is yours? the stranger will ask.
Oh—none. I come here when I'm feeling low.
That's smart, the stranger will say. I'll stay for a while.

Your acquaintance will leave and this woman, you
don't know, will stay

She'll tell you she feels sorriest for sausage dogs
A tube of a torso balanced on teeny limbs—can
you believe that's been inbred from a wolf?!
Then suddenly she'll stand, saying, I gotta go. I
gotta give this guy's wallet back.
That's nice of you.
Yeah. Well. I found it at the bar where I work, and
he has a donor card, so. I'm going to give it back
to him. You should come. We'll have to take two
buses but it'll be fun.

You'll travel with her, out of the city centre you
know well, onto multilane roads you've never seen
before, lined with strip malls
Grim, isn't it? she'll say. But much cheaper out
here.
The odyssey winds you to the suburbs, through
1950s housing projects, as you chart more new
terrain with this person

You will gawk when she tells you about her
culinary experiments with cow heads
You will marvel at her obsession with
entomology—the study of insects
She will name plant species as you pass them and
regale you with tales of playing the fiddle in a
cover band

When you get to the guy's house, he'll ask. Was
there any cash left in the wallet?

No, your new friend says, empathetically.
Never mind. This is great. Thanks.

On your way back into the city, you'll pass an
intimidatingly expensive hotel
Let's get dinner! Your new friend rings the bell for
the bus stop. On me on me. I've recently come into
some cash.
Let's order oysters! she'll say once you're seated.
Do you like oysters?
I've never had one, you'll admit.
Oh, in that case we'll get twelve.

Over this, the most extravagant meal you've ever
had, she'll introduce you to the idea of thirty by 30
Which is to sleep with thirty people by the time
you're 30 years old.
Only at seven yourself, you'll determine to correct
this
You'll toast, to becoming old women who can look
back on your lives and say, I was well-loved...
Well, I fucked a lot of people.

You'll realise, you haven't thought of your broken
heart in at least three hours

Your stomach will twist watching her stuff an
enormous tip into the bill fold
And when you get outside, she'll say, Oh, could
you cover my bus fare?

You'll laugh and spill secrets all the way home
Golden light of sunset and exhaust giving her a
halo

This is definitely not a date
But it's the best date you've ever been on

And before long, she'll be your best friend

Your kindred spirit
You'll be an odd pair, but you'll agree, this is the
kind of friendship immortalised in literature

And together you make a pact to lead interesting lives that
defy convention

Your ambition burns
To do something
You want to do something
Important
Though you have no idea how

You will have passed peak muscle mass
You will produce less melatonin
Your collagen production will be on the decline

There's a moment of pride at not joining the 27-club
Then back to fear

When your brother gets married, your best friend will be your
date to the wedding
At the ceremony you two roll your eyes, but you'll be the last
ones left on the dance floor
Certain you hold the key to living right

Your dad
Is getting old
And you've been angry your whole life that you don't know him
Or, if you're really being honest, that he doesn't know you
You will spend years trying to resign yourself to the fact that
your dad will die

And you'll never really have had a relationship with him
The problem with families? your best friend says. They're too
close to you, to ever fully see you.

You will travel overseas for the first time on your own dime

FIST

You'll overpack and spend most nights on the
couches of friends in shared houses

An amazing coincidence, your dad will be in the
same city, overlapping your stay for four days
Doing research on a lesser-known seventeenth-
century war

On his first night, you'll have him to dinner in the
shared flat, where a childhood friend—nemesis—
lives with her husband
You got along as kids, but you think of her as a
nemesis because you kind of look alike, except
she's always been a little bit prettier, a little bit
faster and exponentially more organised than you
Your childhood nemesis puts your silly
accomplishments to shame with her impressive
career abroad advocating for human rights, and
getting attention

It will be difficult not to self-deprecate in her
presence
And even though you don't want a career like hers,
you'll envy her tangible successes
And you'll hate yourself for that

On another day, you'll book tickets to the theatre,
misunderstand the train's rerouting message, and

WELL IT'A FUNNY HOW KIDS TRY TO DO THINGS THEIR PARENTS WEREN'T ABLE TO DO

end up spending all the money in your pockets on
a taxi
Your dad will be standing in the lobby—with a
clear view of the entrance, watching for you
You'll cry at having kept him waiting

By curtain call, the mounting tightness in your
chest will have you struggling for a deep breath
Dad, you'll say. I feel like there's a fist clenching my
heart.
He'll reply, Hmm. Let's get dinner.

...Now the '45 Rebellion... the whole war was one
25-year-old man's attempt to regain the British
throne for his father...
This is what your dad has been all day in the
archives studying, and will tomorrow too
Wow. What a thing to do, you'll say.
Well, it's funny how kids try to do things their
parents weren't able to do.
How do you mean?
Like you.
Now three or four in, he'll make his confession
If I had my druthers, I'd have the career you're
after.

And you'll wonder, Why? Why did I have to cross an ocean to
learn that?

You'll tear around drunk with your best friend
You'll sing: Mama's planting trees, Mama's growing tall,
Mama's loving hard... and dance in the snow
One night at 4 a.m., you'll dig your fingernails into her waist

when she starts talking about tossing herself into the canal
And the next morning she'll laugh, Aren't I dramatic?

You'll have another health scare
This time it'll be something
You'll recover
But a new appreciation for your body will descend
You'll resolve to drink more water, eat more vegetables and
exercise more
And you will
For a while

At 30 you'll say, I've been thinking of moving away.
Away? Like, this country?
No. Away overseas.
And your best friend will say, I hate it! But you have to go.
You'll go

From afar, you'll watch your friends couple off
Babies will be born
By choice
By design
Sometimes by painstaking effort and expense
By people you never dreamed would have, let alone want, a
baby
You'll be baffled
You're an adult in a romper, wearing a backpack, living in a
shared flat
You'll wonder if you're a perpetual child or existentially a
youth
You'll ask your brother and god
And when neither of their answers are satisfying
You determine that you didn't come here to make a baby

You came here to do something
Important
And you will work, hard

Then:

    Panic, dread and denial will accompany the sightings of
    your first grey hairs
    The aching in your knees as you descend the stairs
    The fine lines that become permanent fixtures on your
    face

Your work will flounder, stumble and slip
The success you hoped for after uprooting yourself will elude you
Your bank account will dwindle
But you'll be too proud to go back home

You'll do nearly everything alone, and hear yourself humming
a few lines of a song your mother sang when you couldn't
sleep
You're not sure if this was a folk song from your grandparents'
country or something your mom invented
The next time she calls, you'll think, I'll ask her.

You'll miss your best friend, only whenever you speak, she's
stoned and distracted

And you'll find yourself yearning for a partner, even though
you'll know that it's all a sham—it's all a way human beings
attempt to make sense of their brutal lives as mammals
You'll know that romantic love is a construct, and that most
people use relationships to give their lives meaning and then
find themselves disappointed
And anyway, you're not like most people
And anyway, you don't want a conventional life

But love will find you
Sitting at the back of a crowded bus

Moving through the stone and chrome financial
district of your new city
You'll agree with your seatmate, Yeah, talking
about meditation is much easier than actually
meditating.
And as the bus stutters up a congested high street,
schoolchildren weaving between vehicles, he'll say,
I've never—uh—I've never—uh—
Done this?
Yeah.

His teeth are stained but his smile's warm
And you'll know he's extremely attractive but
you're not sure that you could you ever be attracted
to someone so attractive

Should we—uh—talk more?
Now?
Sure.
So you'll stay on past your stop and instead travel
with him to a pub he knows the owner of
And you'll snag the snug
And laugh as he recounts the last conversation he
had with his father, before he died
All financial advice and questions about cooking rice
You'll miss your dad
Something fierce for a flash
What's that? He'll ask.
Oh, I just get pangs of homesickness sometimes.
Do you think you'll move back?
Never. Never.

Bus

WORK IS BAD

BUT LOVE IS GOOD

and THAT'S
SOMETHING

The walls of his flat are covered with charcoal
drawings and paintings in progress
He'll have a job he despises but he only wants to
talk about art

I like you, he'll say, as you sway in his kitchen.
What? You'll reply, Why?
You seem very... alive.
You'll caution him not to fall for you—secretly
playing out a long-held fantasy to warn someone
that you are, in fact, 'bad news'
I'm the same as you. The last thing I want is what
everyone else is striving for. I never want a normal
life.

You'll maul each other in the back of cabs
Stand in awe at your opposing accents
Spend mornings after, prowling his
neighbourhood, hungover, gulping coffees
He'll unpick your knotted hair when you pause on
a bench

Moving through this big city with him, a lifer—
born there—reduces it to a small town
He bumps into someone he knows wherever you
go, and he'll hold empirical knowledge of where
to find the best of everything: leather cobblers,
limoncello, mid-century modern furniture

He'll beg you to have sex without turning off the
lights
You'll decline
Except when you're really drunk

He'll ask you to go steady and tell you he loves you
Your heart will wallop your ribcage
You'll want to say it back, but instead you laugh
He'll be undeterred

You'll notice the only finished paintings he has
were all painted by other people
But you'll fold your lives together (sheets of butter
into dough)
He'll moan that you take too long to return his
calls
You'll worry that he drinks a lot

It'll take you a long time for you to profess your love in return
But once you do, you'll think, Okay.
Work is bad but love is good and that's something and I'll take it.
You take it

You will realise you don't enjoy living in a messy house
You will take pleasure in meal prep that doesn't clutter up
your kitchen
At 33, you'll beg your partner to get a dog, he'll say he'd love to
but he's allergic

Then one day, something odd happens
You'll find yourself in a stadium, in your hometown
Your face is sore, though you can't remember why
Your brother is there
And you'll know he's saying something to you, but you can't
hear it
You're too far apart
So you run towards him, and then he starts to run, and
you're running, you hate to run, you're running, chasing your
brother
When you touch your face, there's a hole in your cheek
What? you'll think. I thought we filled this up.
And as you tilt your head

Your teeth fall through the hole in your face
Next thing, you're in the stands and your brother is saying, It's
okay it's okay.
You'll see that he's tied to his chair
And then you feel it
Cold metal O—someone has a gun to your neck
Your brother will contort his face as if to apologise
But you'll know that this is your fault
You can't remember why but you'll know
And you'll start to plead with the gunman
Then the fuzz of your grandparents' TV between channels
and the warmth of your blood between your shoulder blades
You'll bleed out on the concrete stairs
And you'll hear yourself thinking, I love everyone.

In the darkness, a noise
Dripping

You're awake
It's been storming all night
And as you place a bowl under the leak in the ceiling, you'll
wonder why, Why this dream, over and over?

When you ask your brother, he'll say, I think dreams only
recur until you get the message.
But what's the message?
When you mention it to your lapsed Catholic mother, she'll
say, Sweetheart, we have to accept that there are mysteries.

When you visit your best friend, you get drunk together
About the dream, she'll say, You should do acid or ayahuasca.
Get to the bottom of your fear of death.
She'll tell you she's more afraid of life than death. The altered
states make life worth living. Without them, what's the point?

You will meet more grey hairs with resignation
You'll throw your back out doing something innocuous,
like showering

You will get tired of being broke and be tempted to lean on
your partner's affluence
He'll have been imploring you to use the crutch for years
But his stained teeth will have started to irk you
His mother will be clamouring for grandchildren
And though he promised, when you met, that he didn't want
a normal life
He'll be pestering you about when you might want to 'start
trying'
And he'll murmur, You won't ever need to work again.

Then your best friend will do something

HOSPITAL

Someone calls you from the hospital

And you'll find yourself rushing along the
fluorescent-lit corridors
Thrumming with a strange cocktail of fury and
relief, because your best friend's attempt on her
life failed

Your best friend will shrug apologetically when
you enter the room
The curtain pulled around her bed, a flimsy
partition between her and another person on
suicide watch
Her dark eyeliner gone
She looks so
Plain

BUT YOU DON'T LIKE ME RIGHT NOW?

NO I DON'T

You will slide in along beside her
She'll be stiff when you put your arms around her
shoulders
She'll be attached to a drip, so you do this gingerly
As gingerly as you can
Her stomach will have been pumped
Her wrists bandaged

You really wanted to go, you'll say. (Not knowing
what else to do but joke.)
She'll nod
When you'll tilt your head against hers she won't
move away
Which is something, because she's not a hugger
Do you hate me? She'll want to know.
No.
But you don't like me right now.
You'll shake your head. No I don't.
Yeah. Well. Join the club.

When visiting hours are over, you'll stand in
front of the vending machine, dredging out soup
made from powder, remembering that you both
committed to living lives that defied convention
And think, She nearly ended it and I'm nowhere
close.

When you get home, you'll reject your boyfriend's proposal
and move out of the place you share
Anyway, it wasn't so much a proposal as it was an ultimatum
You will turn back to your work
Whispering (to your last few unmarried friends), I feel like I
escaped a collapsing building in the nick of time. So what if
I've got housemates again?

You'll claw your career back
You'll be 35

You'll look at photos of your younger self and be astounded
by the beauty you possessed
You'll lament that you felt like shit at the time those photos
were taken
That you agonised over your zits, that you had a meltdown in
the mirror before leaving the house, that you sucked in your
gut all evening
You'll think: I was perfect! I was perfect. I was perfect.
Why didn't I enjoy it?!
You'll stare at your reflection, in some horrible kaleidoscope
of a fitting room
Aghast to see your mother's bum attached to your body
But you'll like yourself more as time ages you
And age is a feeling
You'll feel it

You'll stop wanting to go to festivals
Or stay out late
Or go out at all

You'll develop a deep irritation with your younger self's
laissez-faire attitude towards the future

You'll regret not flossing your teeth
You'll regret not putting £20 into a savings account each week
You'll mourn the wunderkind you never were

Months will pass during which you and your best friend play
phone tag
Only you're relieved every time she doesn't answer
And you let her calls go to voicemail
When you do speak, she's preoccupied and you're impatient

Then nothing
Silence between you
For years
You're not sure if you were the last, or if she was, to reach out
You'll worry that she's died
But with no news from her stepsister, you'll trust she's alive
You'll miss your friend
And you'll hate her too

Still it stays with you, the question of how—or what she will
remember of you

And you'll get it, anew:
Even your closest confidante
Will only ever know a handful of truths about you

You'll figure out a way to stop living hand to mouth—to live
'comfortably'
You won't respect your newfound income stream
But you'll take it

Your dad will send you songs by the forgotten greats
Emails with loving sentiments about audacious harmonies
Lyrics about the old men in the spring

On his birthday, your dad will tell you, Getting older is a
series of rapid physical adaptations.
It's like being a baby.
Learning to move through the world with a body that's swiftly
changing.

In the span of one week, two seismic emails will arrive

The first one is from your best friend—old best
friend—the one you met in the dog park
You haven't spoken in—how long is it? Two years.
More?
Saying, Hello Stranger. I tried to off myself again.
You'll want to respond
In your mind, you'll pen impassioned replies, that
say: I think about you. All. The. Time.
But you'll stay quiet
She's an addict, your brother warns. Do you really
think anything you say will make her change?
Trust me, don't engage. It'll only cause pain.

You'll feel guilty for your hard line
But hold it
You'll delete her email

And as you do that, the second email will arrive

It's from your childhood nemesis—the one you
stayed with on your first trip abroad, prettier,
faster, more accomplished
She'll be living in another country now, a place
you've always considered equally exotic and
sophisticated
She'll be fluent in their local dialect, not only
married, divorced and remarried, with a daughter
and a position as a tenured professor

She's writing to tell you that she's just been
diagnosed with cancer

You'll be ashamed for all the times you wished that
she'd fail

A few weeks later, they'll remove tumours and a
couple weeks after that she'll begin chemotherapy
Posting a picture telling people to enjoy her
mermaid locks while they last

When you call to check in, she'll say, I'm watching the oranges fall off the tree in the garden. The only annoying thing is that I can't make marmalade this year.

She'll make a video joyously shaving her head with her daughter
You will be spooked by her determinedly optimistic approach
She will be endlessly positive and supportive, celebrating your petty work-related 'victories'

Months later, your childhood nemesis with cancer will call to say the cancer's spread and her husband has left her
What a rebirth, she'll exclaim.

You're not far away so you'll get on a plane, and stay with her for a week
You won't see the country though; you'll see hospitals
You'll see tangerine paint on the headboards and doorways, a distraction from the bodies filled with chemicals and instruments, anything to keep them above ground
You and your old nemesis will talk a lot
She'll tell you her second husband was having an affair throughout their entire marriage, with a younger woman—A cliché but true.
You'll say, We don't know anyone. We don't know anyone, do we?
Well, I'm sure you have secrets you've kept from me too.
Alright, you'll admit. Our whole lives I've been jealous of you.
Until now, she'll retort. And when your face loses colour, she'll laugh.

She'll ASK IF YOU BELIEVE IN the AFTERLIFE

YOU'LL MOVE YOUR MOUTH AROUND A LOT

Oh, I'm awful.
Nah. We contain multitudes.

And you'll know she's right. No one can ever know
everything about you—not even yourself

You'll take her 6-year-old daughter out for meals.
She'll talk your ear off about birds of prey and then
refuse to speak
She'll ask if you believe in the afterlife
You'll move your mouth around a lot, stalling
And she'll say, Because I do.
And so you'll agree, I do too.

And then you'll fly home.

You'll tell yourself, You've got to find a way not to think about
these two friends. All. The. Time.
You'll ask your brother and god
And when neither of their answers are satisfying
You'll walk through the cemetery near your flat
Hoping for a profound message from the dead
But mostly find yourself scanning the gravestones for baby
names
You'll think, What's the point of procreating if we all end up
here?
And the dead will answer back something about housing a
soul

You'll wonder, Why didn't I invest more in skin care?

You'll lose hours, scrutinising your skin in the mirror, pulling
loose flesh back to reveal your former self

Your teeth will shift

You'll be incensed
Nobody warns you that your teeth shift—well, your teeth
shift!—and suddenly your tongue feels different in your
mouth
(A true sign that time will ravage your physical form)

You'll resolve to drink more water, eat more vegetables and
exercise more
And you will
For a while

And you will work. Hard.

Every time you leave the city you live in, for whatever reason
You'll send your nieces a postcard
Embellishing your adventures

You will blame your parents
You'll blame your genetics
You'll blame your brother
Your exes
Before you blame yourself
You will blame yourself
For all the things you haven't done that you've wanted to do
Because after all, the common denominator is you

You'll have a breakthrough at work and no one will notice

Your childhood nemesis with cancer will recover and then the
cancer will come back
Can I go and see her? you'll think.
But before you figure out the right weekend and book the
flights, she's gone
39
She was 39 and now you're 40
She'll leave you her record collection

You'll get on a plane and pick it up
Her ex will say you can't see their daughter—it's not clear
why—so you'll send her some money—not enough
And her records will sit in a box in the corner of your bedroom
Screaming that life is short and—
All you can think of are baby names

Your dad will write his first and only book—a biography

BOOK

Beavering away day after day for several years
And through a friend, get it into the hands of an
editor
And now, in his late 70s, he's a published
biographer
The subject matter is secondary to the fact that it's
done and published

You will fly home for the launch
Your dad will give a speech and mention you—
well, the children, of which you're one—but barely
Fair enough, you think.
You and your brother were impediments to
everything he actually wanted to do
How much can he thank you, when he doesn't?

Nervous to read pages from the book, when your
dad falters, tripping up on a word, he'll apologise,
sincerely
And it's just a tiny moment, but it's as though he's
apologising for existing, for being human, as if
being fallible is a disgrace
You'll wish you could replace his backbone with a
steel rod
You'll clap loud and stand up straight on his behalf

WHAT SENDS

OUR ANIMAL

UNDERGROUND?

Afterwards, last ones to leave a party, you'll be
sitting with your dad
And without prompting he'll tell you that when
he was 6 years old, at the now long-gone family
cottage, he was playing with a friend—and the
friend fell off the dock and got stuck underwater
Neither boy had learned how to swim
And your dad tried desperately to scream for help
but all that came out was a whisper

Help!
His voice hollow in his throat
And his friend, under the water
Scrambling, flailing
And your dad's legs wouldn't move
No adults in sight
Just trees rocks water
And his voice
Was hollow
Help!

Then the dock shook, there was a splash, his
friend's older brother was in the lake, pulling his
younger brother up, holding him to his chest as
he swam backwards to shore, hoisting him over
his shoulder, thwacking his back, the little boy
coughing up water, crying, shaking

Your dad, a child, watching his friend revived

That's horrifying, Dad.

Your dad will move his empty wine glass in circles
on the table and say, Mmm. Yeah. It was really
something.

You will think of this anecdote over and over

You will wonder what happened to your dad that by
age 6 he couldn't scream
What sends our animal underground?
You'll think, My child will never lose their voice.
My child would scream like hell. My child will stay
an animal. My child. I have to have a child. I could
really raise a good one. I could raise a good one.

Oh god.

This biological imperative thrums in you
This month? This month? This month?

You will be aching
Dreaming
To *will* new life into this world
The same way you were willed into existence
Through science and love
Or was it god?

You'll have the dream again
Awake, sweating, sweeping your tongue around your mouth
Making sure you've still got all your teeth

You will scour for a mate
You'll be 43
But everyone you date will be miles from the intensity you
felt at the back of that bus
And you'll know what people say
'Love changes as you age'
But you won't want to enter something passionless

So you'll decide to do it on your own

You will employ science

You will spend the money you've earned
Pursuing your deafening instinct to procreate before it's too
late

E G G S

You'll suffer through confounding meetings with
nurses and doctors who speak too fast and assume
you understand jargon you don't
They'll test your AMH and FSH and give you a
transvaginal ultrasound
Your follicle reserve is great, they'll say.
Hope!
And your grandmother gave birth to your mother
at 40?
Yes.
More hope!

Look. Eggs get weaker and meeker as we age, a
nurse says bluntly. So don't feel bad if your eggs
aren't great.

To work on your egg quality, you'll employ a
holistic nutritionist
She'll have you take CoQ10, Omega 3s, folic acid
and fat soluble D3

After your period comes and goes, you'll begin
injecting yourself with synthetic oestrogen
Always squeamish with needles, you'll fight your
gag reflex, sitting on the edge of the bathtub,
trying to decide whether a subcutaneous jab would
be easier in your abdomen or thigh
It'll take two hands to steady the syringe
And won't be sure that you did it right

But two days later
You are all

you are all

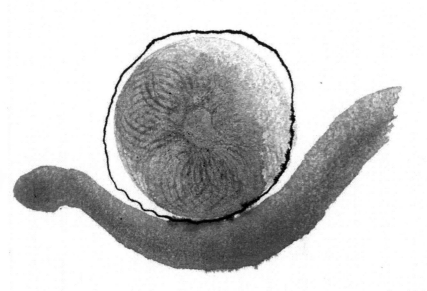

MOOD MOOD
MOOD MOOD
MOOD MOOD MOOD

MOOD MOOD MOOD MOOD MOOD MOOD
MOOD
Can't stop crying

Then harvesting
The doctor will insert the long needle into your
cervix and extract thirteen eggs!
They'll harvest thirteen eggs!
Hope.

Then embryos will be made with your donor's
sperm—you picked him based on his interests in
cosmology and hot sauce—two subjects about
which you know very little

Only four embryos will survive the first week
Then they'll test the embryos to see if they'd be
viable pregnancies
And none are viable
A nurse will tell you this over the phone and ask if
you'd like to do another round
Try again?

Five rounds later, your resources drained and a few
implantations that don't take
Your womb will be deemed a hostile place

And after some kitchen-floor sobbing

You'll hear yourself saying, That'll do pig, that'll do.

You'll work hard

You'll love your nieces with a fervour you hadn't thought possible
You will delight in watching them grow
And be glad that your life hasn't been overrun by doing dishes
and never having more than forty seconds to reflect

And besides, you'll tell yourself, the world doesn't need us to have children—it doesn't—it doesn't.
You'll tell yourself, Your love and care aren't wasted if you don't have a copy of your DNA out there. Come on.

At 44, you will have sex that is dirty and kinky and comforting and bottom of the lake, cervix knocking, spiritual touching of god glorious
And it'll make you feel young, but you'll know you couldn't have done it like that when you were young because age, time and experience have made you bold, honest and wise about what actually turns you on

> You will find a white pubic hair
> You will find that pepper and tomatoes make your tongue patchy, and give them up
> You'll give into vanity and cut dairy and beer from your diet without fuss

You'll find that you've designed a life that is one part what you want, and one part a prison of duties and obligation and playing a version of yourself you've twice outgrown but can't outrun
You'll go to therapy, meditate, read self-help books and you'll escape the prison you constructed
And then build another one—less severe but still—
Only to escape that, and so on
And so on and so on

And each time
You'll resolve to drink more water, eat more vegetables and exercise more
And you will
For a while

And you will spend unconscionable amounts of money trying
to stay young...

Thousands will be spent on:

Dental work
Face cream
Moisturiser
Vitamins
Microneedling
Chemical peels

Pilates
Yoga
Facials
Retinol
Hair dye
An exercise bike

Hyaluronic acid
Cosmetic acupuncture
A cold plunge pool
Ecstatic dance
Personal trainers
Collagen powder

Face masks
Tennis lessons
Teeth bleaching

None of it works.

Your father dies
And you won't make it home in time
It was awful, your mother will say.

He'd died, separated from us, by machinery that was meant to keep him alive.
She'll keep pausing in the middle of rooms, turning to you and saying, You know, he wasn't perfect, but he was a really good guy.
And she'll cry for thirty seconds, bony shoulders shaking, and then keep moving
Your mother's house, your childhood home, fills up with flowers
So many that when you stumble to the bathroom in the middle of the night
You'll wonder if the flowers are growing out of the floorboards

You'll think of all the things you never knew about your dad
You'll recall him saying, about the biography he published, There's so much that I missed.
And you thought, Dad, it's five hundred pages.
You'll wonder if he ever worried about missing too much of your life
You'll wonder why he stopped emailing you songs
You'll wonder if in some ways he hated you
Or if he was giving you a pass—total freedom to live without owing him anything
Not even a reply to an email

You'll wake up earlier and earlier without an alarm
You'll have a renewed sense of carpéing your diems
You'll wonder if it was right to reject the proposal, from the guy you met at the back of that bus
Because it seems no one is really *that* happy in their marriage
Is it really better to be alone?

Your old best friend darts through your mind

You'll remember sitting on the edge of the dog park with her
Should I have reached out? you'll wonder.
Worry looms
And guilt worms itself into your lungs

You'll settle into what your life is—contained
You will work hard
You'll earn better money
You'll start giving advice to people because they're asking for it
You won't understand why, but find you have something to say, and so you say things like:

Don't succumb to cynicism.
Wear comfortable shoes.
Say 'No' more often. No need to stay busy for busy's sake.
Relax. There is not a finite amount of talent.
Stretch often. Even if you feel embarrassed, do it. Do it at work. Do it now, before it's too late and you have permanent back problems.

The 25-year-olds won't take it, but at 49, you'll know it's sage
And you will wish you had listened when you were that age

An email will come—
A message to you from an old flame—the one you met at the back of that bus—the one whose proposal you refused fifteen years ago. He's in town for work

TEETH

Can we meet?
Sure.

You want to look good but primping in the mirror, distinctly feels like polishing up an old, broken toy

In the pub
You'll see
He's angry
He's angrier now and his voice, more congested
His teeth, more stained
He still puts beer back, fast

He'll tell you about his divorce
He'll tell you about his wedding day, and the panic
attack he had
It was a train moving too fast, jumping off would
have maimed me.

By your second round, you'll be reminiscing about
the time you two whiled away together at bars, on
beaches, in basements... talking...

We talked so much, he'll say. I've never talked with
someone so much since.
And you'll think, Well, you did slightly more
talking than I did, but fine.
What did we talk about?
Well, we were—
Young.
We weren't *that* young.
No. We were... that was...

You lock eyes
He'll tell you he regrets proposing in the way he
did
You'll try to brush it off
I was an idiot, he'll say—I was pushing for
something I thought would...
Never mind. It's okay.

When you leave, the summer evening embraces
you and fall into his chest and breathe a scent

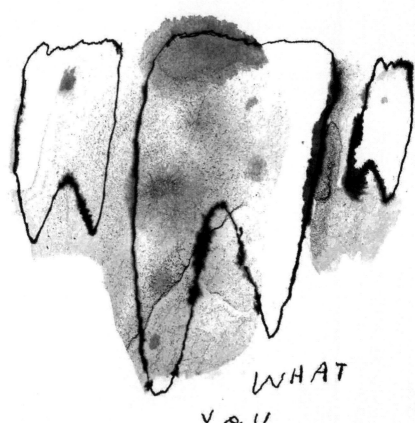

you'd forgotten that transports you back to
hungover mornings prowling his neighbourhood
and a younger version of you

You'll kiss at the station entrance, first on cheeks,
then lips, linger a little longer than—
And when he starts to whisper something into
your neck, you pull away, squeeze his tricep and
nod

And you'll get it
It's about knowing that if you wanted to you could
It's about knowing that doors you thought were
boarded up
Can always be pried open
And knowing that together is hotter than
whatever clumsy, gulping, mashing of flesh might
have passed

It was nice seeing you.
It was

But he isn't now what you remember then

This person
This towering person
Now is just normal, mortal
You'll think, Why did I love you?
Why did my heart wallop my ribcage?
Why did I prize you so high?

You will work, hard
You will bury some hatchets and some hopes
You will watch your friends age
You'll take note of who's doing it well and who's doing it badly
And when it seems they're all doing it well, you'll wonder if
you're the turkey

You'll ask your brother and god
And when neither of their answers are satisfying
You'll resolve to drink more water, eat more vegetables, and
exercise more
And you will
For a while

Your friends' parents die
Your friends get sick
Your friends get divorced, some of them for a second time
One for a third
People in your life move away, go to AA, become addicted to
gardening, running marathons, solving crossword puzzles
People in your life pivot 180 degrees and become landlords
You and your current partner pass judgement on these
changes as you amble through the park near your home

Your mother dies
Her soft hands are stiff and cold by the time you touch them
Her lips purple
Her mouth slightly open
Your brother sells your childhood home, and you give your
share to his daughters
Why not?
But also, if ever someone had to take you in... they might

With your mother gone
You'll float above your life, some desolate balloon
You won't dare take a deep breath
As each time you do, your diaphragm touches your grief and
levels you

Months after her funeral you'll hum it
You never got around to asking your mom what that tune was
from

A jingle? Some hymn she learned in her youth?
And you'll curse all the ways you convinced yourself your
mom would live forever
And you'll wail for the better part of an afternoon
Until you wipe your snot on your sleeve
And you hear her voice saying, Oh sweetheart, get up. Go
outside!

You'll leave the house faster
You'll stop caring so much what other people think of your
tatty boots, your nasal voice, your unkempt hair
You'll take your time looking for the correct change even if
there's a line forming behind you
You'll tell strangers who are crying in public, It's going to be
okay. And when they tell you, You don't know what you're
talking about, you'll concede, No, I don't. Then you'll carry on
with your day and never think of them again
At 52, you'll go on vacation alone, without your partner, and it
will completely renew your relationship
You will relish solitude
You'll sleep less
But you'll dream more about people who have died
You'll wake up and say it was so real, it was so real, it was so
real.
You'll be nostalgic for the things that were popular in your
teenage years
When a colleague says, You know, the older I get, the better I
was, you'll laugh.
You know you also glorify your youth, and also, you can't help
it
You miss the sense of possibilities
You miss the hope that age would answer your unanswered
questions

But of course, age is only a feeling
(You feel it)

You'll ache to apologise for all the times you hurt your parents
That time, waiting for the train with your mom, crying,
because something she'd done to help you, made you furious
I live to make you happy.
Well don't Mom.
But you'll know now that you'd have parented like that too
What's the alternative?

You'll scare yourself losing your temper with your partner
when he suggests selling your flat and moving out of the city
together
I'm too old. I can't.
And when he gets snide and cold, you'll push him away
Get out.
You'll be alone

Going to visit your family, you'll end up on an airplane...

PLANE

Normally, you do whatever it takes to avoid a
chatty seatmate, but this time will feel different

He'll be a young man, broad-shouldered, calloused
hands, neat haircut
Fingers interlaced in his lap

He'll ask if you're going home or visiting
That's a tricky one, you'll say.
He'll tell you he's going home
He was away on military business
He's high up now
Training and administrating things

But two tours behind him
You'll prod. You can't help it. Did you see action?
Yes.
How did you—can I ask—how did you get your
head around the possibility that, at any moment,
you could have died?
Uh. He'll sigh and tap the window with the
knuckle of his index finger. Do you want the
answer I normally give people? Or the answer-
answer?
I want the answer-answer.

'kay. There were a few times I thought my ticket
was gonna be punched, he'll say. And I'm an
atheist, so no paradise for me.
Then one night in the desert, I got it:
Death isn't good or bad, right? It's neutral, like
nature. When you die, you will feel nothing,
because there is nothing. And when there is
nothing, there's nothing to fear.
And that.
Carried me.

But you're glad you lived?
Oh, god yeah.

You'll nod and feel compelled to thank him for his
service, even though you're a pacifist
Even though you believe the industry of war is vile
All you'll manage to get out is, I'm glad too.

Halfway across the ocean, after four rye and
gingers, he'll tell you about the smells that follow
him—even though he lost his ability to smell—the
acrid smell of cordite, the coppery smell of blood,
the sweet smell of rotting flesh, the overcooked
pork smell of burning flesh, the smell of faeces

ONE NIGHT IN the DESERT I GOT IT

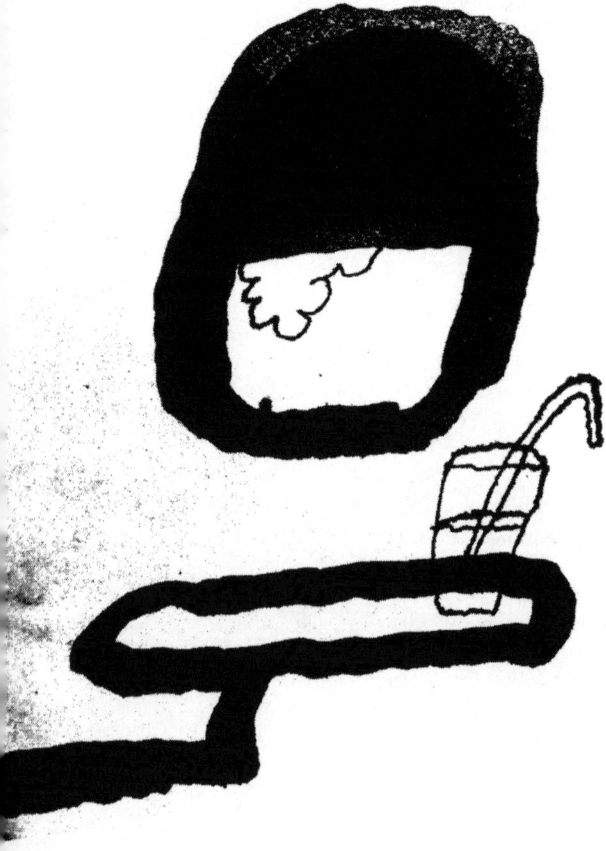

because of a round through someone's intestines,
or someone's bowels gave way through fear, or
pain, or 'cause they died.

He'll tell you about watching his best friend die
How his best friend cried out for his mother
He'll say, You'd be amazed how many young troops
call for their moms at the end.

You'll feel sorry for yourself, never being anyone's mother—
never needed in a moment of despair

And then you'll torpedo backwards, your myopic view will
expand, and you'll know just what a tiny speck you are

You'll have the dream again
Only you're lucid this time
And turn to face the gunman
And it's you
Really? You'll think. Come ON.
A colleague who's done Jungian analysis will say, Well, I hate
to tell you, but the psyche is rarely subtle.

You'll work hard
You'll love to work
You'll wonder if your work has been of value to anyone but you
You'll dwell on the futility of your life's contribution...
You'll ask your brother and god
And when neither of their answers are satisfying
You conclude that there's nothing else you could do at this
point
So you host people for meals where you say things like, Oh
that was a hundred years ago—remember that!? Remember
that. Remember that... You know, I had completely forgotten.

Your oestrogen levels will plummet
Your ovaries and uterus will shrink
Your now fibrous breasts droop down your front

And just like you witnessed—you'll be throwing open
windows in the coldest months, too hot, flushed, praying for a
swift transition of your hormones

Your weight will redistribute itself, yet again
Your periods will stop

You'll live without the monthly reminder of time passing

You'll resign yourself to the reality that just because you work
hard doesn't mean you're entitled to wild success
You did good work, you did, you did good work
You worked hard and you did good work
You'll accept that the world is not a meritocracy
You'll think, Okay. I didn't have a child and I didn't make a
family and I didn't gain the recognition I'd hoped for with
all my hard work. Okay—no buts. Just, okay. Okay. Enough
lashing myself for not getting more.
At 56, you'll let go of wanting more
And you'll feel lighter
And you'll wish you'd done it three decades before

You didn't
You don't know why
You are getting better though
At accepting what you know
And what you won't

You always wanted a dog

But someone close to you was always allergic
You'll be single again
And of a certain age

You will wait your turn in the queue, slap down
top dollar and you get a dog!
A dog! A dog!
Your own dog

You get a dog and not just any dog, a puppy

A black lab with a shimmering coat and intelligent
eyes

Your colleagues will shower you with treats
You'll blow your monthly budget on his bed and
bowl and lead
You'll shell out for the most expensive food
Honest to god, you love your dog
Your dog!
Your dog

And you knew it wouldn't be easy raising a puppy
but when he pees and poos indoors four times a
day you won't be fazed

You'll let him sleep in your bed
You'll let him gnaw on the sofa
You'll be besotted
When you go to the supermarket without him,
you won't be able to wait to get back home to
that sweetie, who just wants to command your
attention

You'll be eager to dote

His training will go poorly
You'll be too indulgent

And you'll have mixed feelings about obedience
school—you'll want him to be well-trained so you
can take him everywhere, but you also won't want
him cowering without a personality

Never before a morning person, you'll anticipate
the 6 a.m. wake-up—and be out in the
neighbourhood as dawn cracks
Walking your dog!
Your dog

He'll love everything: candy-bar wrappers, coffee
cups, poo bags, birds—oh god, birds—little kids

He'll be so keen to jump up on a stroller

He won't listen
But he'll like to run

You'll have a retractable leash
You'll be getting the hang of
It seemed like a good compromise
You'll still be struggling with what should be
simple technology
Simple technique
But you'll get confused about what to press to
pause the release

And then on a Saturday afternoon, you'll be out for
a walk

Your dog will be getting bigger
You'll think of him as a teenager now

And the dog sees a bird and darts and you fumble
with the leash and the bus crests the hill and
swerves to get around a parked car and a car
coming from other direction honks because of the

HONEAT TO GOD

YOU LOVE YOUR DOG

buses' wide berth and you're fumbling with the
leash and the leash is ripped from your hand and
there's a thud and you can't see your dog
Your dog
You can't see your dog

You scream his name and see blood in the road
The bus and the car stop and a man walking on
the sidewalk turns back and runs into the middle
of the street and scoops up your dog and brings
him to the curb

Your dog
You'll see his brain on the road
Your dog
Your dog

And all you can do is caw and clutch your knees
and sob

People will get out of their cars and ask if he's okay
He's gone! you'll shout
He's gone.

They'll ask if they can call someone
And your screams will come out rhythmically
You won't know you're shaking until someone
wraps a fleece blanket around your shoulders
It smells like someone else's dog
You'll scream caw sob

You hear yourself saying:

Please, this can't happening.
Please, don't let this be happening.

You'll shake on the side of the road
Groups of people congregate and disperse

You'll cover your mouth and bend your knees
The bus will leave
The lady will get back in her car

And your dog
Your dog
Your dog

You'll want to die
You'll want to obliterate yourself
You'll do it in the only way you're not afraid
You'll drink

Your tears will come in torrents
So many
You'll wonder if all these tears really are just for your dog?
Never mind, you'll think.
You'll drink some more

And somehow

After four weeks of a vodka haze and weight loss and a
fridge filled with rotting vegetables and unwashed hair and
unbrushed teeth
Your mother's voice takes hold of you—Keep moving.

So
You will find a meeting
You'll be silent
But you'll keep going and slowly, waking up in the mornings
won't be the most unbearable
Your appetite will creep back
You will be able to focus for an hour at a time

After meetings, you'll get coffee with the same person, over
and over
He's the only person you've met who truly thinks before
speaking
And his favourite phase is, Let's see.
He'll be devoted to his garden and his grown-up children
His reverence for Olympic athletes will be delightfully
mockable
He'll laugh at your self-deprecation but not without making a
point of gently disagreeing
And two years later, you'll have fallen in love
You will find it
You will have found it again
At 60 it will be the opposite to the frenetic fireworks of past
loves
It will be steady, undeniable
An ocean liner—slow-moving, unstoppable, unsinkable
Everyone should do this late in life, you'll think.

Your partner's hands will be wrinkled

　　You will be flirting with osteoporosis

But your love life has never been—
Inhibitions gone, tenderness abounds—

How lucky are we? you'll both say.

And leaving work one day, you'll hear your name called

DINER

You turn
It's me.
Your cheeks will go slack, and your stomach will
thump
Hi.

It's your old best friend
The one you met in the dog park
The one you visited in hospital on suicide watch
You haven't had contact in thirty-one years

There's a place around the corner—
A diner—
We can—they won't rush us out—
It's loud but not deafening—
I'm a little deaf now.

You'll sit across from each other

Her dark eyeliner just the same
Her earlobes longer
A scar on her neck you won't remember

I'm sorry to spring myself on you.

They'll bring her a coffee and you a soda water
She'll tell you she hasn't had a drink in twelve years
You'll tell her you don't drink any more either—
that you met your partner in AA
She'll say she bloomed late but finally landed a job
in entomology
She'll say she's got a cat and the cat's everything
She'll say after a two-decade break she picked up
her fiddle again
Remember the night we sang, Mama's hopes are
high, Mama's fear is loud, Mama's changing course,
Mama's wooing crowds, and it snowed?

Yes... How to catch up on thirty years?
We're old now.
65.
65. God, we're old.

And you'll be thinking, How do we round this?
How do we... Can you salvage something this far
gone?

My stepsister died, suddenly, she'll say. We were
still estranged. And it got me thinking about other
people who—Anyway, you meant a lot to me and
I'm sorry that I was such a mess and that I did
things to drive you away.
No, I'm sorry—
Please, no. I was a wreck.
You'll reach out over the red-top table and grip
her wrist. I think—I still think about you. All. The.
Time.
She'll nod vigorously, blinking
I'm sorry I was a coward. I'm sorry I don't know
how to talk now. I want the lowdown on your love
life, and to ask if you've read x, y and z and get *your*
take on the political buffoons running this place.
Well, ditto ditto.

You'll sit there a long time after your plates are
cleared
You can tell, you both want this to be a
monumental reunion
But neither of you dares rehash the past
And so there is nothing operatic
No tears fall
No heads are held on chests
No great proclamations of forgiveness are made

Just apologies in halting half-measures and relief
You'll know it's better this way, and will yourself
not to be underwhelmed
But you are

Until the bill comes, and just like she did forty
years ago, your old friend says, On me on me, and
stuffs a disproportionately generous tip into the
fold.

Not long after, an epistolary relationship takes
hold.

You exchange letters—emails—and sometimes calls
You'll cackle about how your bodies have changed

You'll find yourself, tying back apron strings
About to pickle beets
Something your mother did
Which you hated—the smell and the taste
And now, dropping beets into brine
You'll watch your purple hands become your mother's

Five years after your meal in the diner
Your old best friend will call in the middle of the night, I'm in
trouble.
And you'll find yourself wending through the fluorescent-lit
halls of a hospital again
70
Heaving yourself onto her hospital bed

She's on her way out
You weren't an angel, she'll say, but you got it. And that's—

When you hug her, she won't just allow it but plant a smack
on your cheek
Don't feel bad for the years we didn't speak. Don't. But can
you find a good home for my cat?
Oh, your partner will say. We'll keep her.

Your partner's kids have kids, and so you get to be a step-
grandma and it's the best and it's also not everything it's
cracked up to be

Your partner encourages you to retire on your own terms
Whatever you want, babe.
He'll insist on eating in restaurants several nights a week—
neither of you like to cook
He'll say, We've got to enjoy ourselves, come on. We can't
afford not to now.
And when you shy away from items on the menu you've never
heard of, he'll say, Let's see. Let's give it a try.
You'll weep with laughter when, impatient, having already
invented an elaborate bedtime story for his grandchildren,
they beg for another and he says, Alright, one more: A fly was
born. It flew around. And then it died. Good night!
You'll hate that no matter how much you talk, you'll never
know everything about his life

You'll bury more friends
You'll push back death with meditation, and medication
If I can live less distractedly, I can savour life better.

Your brother gets ill
And dies
And it's cataclysmic
Awful

But he was old and so are you and what more do you want to wring from this time?
Still

You'd like to stick around to see a few more springs
74 and you and your partner have a list of places to visit
You resolve to drink more water, eat more vegetables and exercise more
And you will
For a while
And you'll go on some trips—one to a nude beach
Why not? you'll shriek.
And you'll skinny dip in broad daylight

You'll regret all the sex you had with the lights off because you were self-conscious of your body
You'll regret that you went so many years without eating croissants when you love butter
You'll regret being stingy with your money and time and not visiting your dad that winter he fell on the ice and broke his hip
You'll regret not telling off people who you knew were in the wrong just because they were older than you

You wish you knew then what you know now: That age doesn't equal intelligence or morality
Age is merely a feeling—you'll feel it—a sense of what's to come
You've witnessed patterns play out many times now
You can't foresee the future, but you can feel it rushing towards you

You'll sleep more
You'll consider a DNR—a 'do not resuscitate' order

You'll try to talk to your family about your DNR at the rare
occasions you're gathered, but your brother's daughters shout
you down
And you think, Come on, girls, this is not what I paid for.
You'll get a DNR written into a document and strong-arm a
few key people into learning its location

Your partner starts to die
He is aware of his death

And he begs that they not hop him up on
morphine
Better to be in pain and present then go out in a
haze.

You will notice sometimes his breathing stops
when he's asleep
A nurse will explain this means he's dipping into
unconsciousness
This will happen more.

He'll tell you, one late afternoon, sun glinting
through the window, that he is enjoying his death
You'll squeeze his hand and laugh and kiss his
temple
And crawl onto the bed—the one you've moved
into the living room—the place he's decided he
wants to die—and sit beside him

The cat will jump up and fold herself into a loaf, in
a square of sunlight at your feet

He will tell you about his father and nod off

The next day he'll be out of bed before you wake
Making bacon and eggs

CRABAPPLE

Listening to Motown
He'll say he finally feels rested
He'll say he wants to get the seedlings in the
ground today
He'll say, Let's go to the nursery too, I want to
plant a new tree.

You'll be worried that he'll crash but he'll insist this
is what he wants to do and so you'll capitulate
Okay, honey. Whatever you say.
His lips, still shiny from the grease of the food, will
curl around his favourite coffee mug

You'll wheel him through the garden centre
He'll pick out a crabapple tree
In your back garden you'll ease seedlings into the
newly thawed earth
And though you disagree about the placement,
you'll plant the tree where he thinks it would be
happiest
You'll wipe your muddy hands on your jeans

After dinner, he's tired

He'll lie in bed
You'll do the dishes
And when the kitchen is gleaming, you'll sit beside
him
He'll be breathing lightly, slowly
And then it'll stop
And then light and slow
And stops
There's still soil under his fingernails
Light and slow
And slow
And slow
And then he opens his eyes and sees you

It's just the two of you in the room
You'll kiss his hand
And he'll reassure, It's okay, it's okay, it's okay.
And he'll nod at you
And you nod back
And he'll reach out his finger and you'll know to
take his hand
And he'll close his eyes
And light and slow
And lighter
And slower
And stops

And you'll wait for him to start breathing again
And you'll wait
And you'll wait
And you'll wait

And you'll know
And it will be so
Quiet
You'll touch your forehead to his

It will be okay
It is

You'll make the calls
You'll make arrangements
You'll think you hear him on the stairs
You'll donate his clothes...

You'll decide to sell your house
But not until after next spring
You want to see the crabapple tree in full bloom again

In the meantime, you'll begin the process of sorting through
all the paper you've amassed
Receipts upon receipts
And you will be frustrated that you can't remember more
things that happened with your partner, while you're flooded
with memories from way, way back...

You will remember crying after a bad haircut when you were
7, powerless in the chair while it was happening
You will remember the bus you took home from high school
and how the hockey players taunted the kid with learning
difficulties in the big green coat and you did nothing—
terrified to intervene and become the new target
You will remember the bedroom you slept in, with the
fireplace, when you were 20 and think, I've never slept in a
room so nice since
You will remember your dad weeping when he found out you
weren't a virgin any more
You'll remember the dream where your teeth fell through
your face and you died thinking, I love everyone, but you can't
remember the last time you had it
You'll remember the summer you were 8, calling up to the
lifeguard, in her tall white chair, I don't want to go in the sea.
And her saying, Go. Wade in. I've got the long view.
You'll remember eating an entire peach-flavoured lip
balm when you were tiny, perched on the toilet in your
grandparents' house
You'll remember your brother yelling at you, You keep men
around for entertainment and you need to change!
You'll laugh
And you'll say out loud, as if to your brother, though he's long
dead, I have changed, by the way.

When all your papers are neatly sorted into piles, you'll look
at them and think, What the fuck am I keeping any of this
for?
And you'll take them out to the barrel, and burn them
The neighbours' boys will come over and run around the fire
And for a second, you'll feel thrilled
Because you know your partner would have laughed his face
off

You'll make it to spring
You'll throw out your partner's toothbrush, but hold off
putting your house on the market for another year, or three...
or
Spring comes again

And at 82
You'll join a choir
Belt out the alto line
But it's mostly just the same note
You'll think, I'm great at this. Why did I convince myself I
couldn't sing harmony?

Every lapse in memory will send you into a spiral, bargaining
with the gods, Never let my brain become mash potatoes...
but spare my knees too!

At 86 you'll move into an assisted-living home
You'll be popular there
A shock
Never having been popular in school
You'll think, Well, at least my life made me interesting.
When the gossip bores you, you'll get up and walk away
And it'll only make the other residents respect you more
What a hoot, you'll think.

What a racket I bought into before.

Your bladder will have lost its elasticity

You'll move slowly but think clear and that's something when you're surrounded by people who've become strangers to their own histories

The days are short and the years—

You'll get your diagnoses and turn 88

You'll remember waking up on your 25th birthday
Your taut skin taken for granted
Bemoaning tiny flaws in your creamy-faced, plump-lipped,
clear-eyed, deep-bending-kneed, hangover-free body

You'll remember your dad saying, 25. That's the age your adult life really begins. Your child brain, finally matured. That's why at 25 they'll finally let you rent a car.

You'll remember the flowers and the message, culled from the cemetery, for you

You'll remember all the things your ambition burned to do, and all the fears you carried about your life being ripped from you too soon

You'll remember you

Before all the parallel lives you could have lived started playing alongside your day-to-day existence, crowding your head, causing you to question if you really did choose well? Did you choose at all? Was there any design? And all the 'Oh but what ifs'—and 'Oh never minds'.

You'll hear someone saying, It's okay.

It is okay
Now that death's nearby, you'll feel more curious than afraid

One of your niece's *daughters* will come to visit
Tell me about you you you, you'll say. Tell me everything
about your life.
Determined not to be one of those ancient people who
drones on about the past
And your niece's daughter obliges you
And it's marvellous
But it's also a little bit dull
And you can't help but think, She's leaving out all the juicy
stuff!

From the next room, you'll hear her hum it—those lines from
the song your mother sang
She'll say she learned it from her mom but doesn't know
where *she* learned it from

At 90, you'll get used to your body being treated as a medical
specimen
Accustomed to needle-prick marks in the crook of your
elbows
Time in waiting rooms
You'll get good at talking to doctors
You'll chuckle that so much of your little time left is spent
waiting

Spring comes again, and...
You will not be resuscitated

You are dead
You died

You are spoken about in the past tense

Your body immaterial
Your belongings distributed, discarded

When the people who knew you talk of you, they'll talk of
your early years
They'll show photos of you as a youngster
Even though most of what you enjoyed most will have
happened after those moments were captured with a flash
This is how you'll be remembered, here, now, at 25
Even though, you have all this to come

And things only you knew will die along with you

People betray themselves
Wars are fought
The crabapple tree blooms in the spring, for a while
For a while you are remembered
And then you're not

So, happy birthday

This message is for you
Here, now, at 25
And at 35, and 42, and 58, and 63, and 70, 80, on:

Age is a feeling you have, you have to look forward to.

PERFORMANCE NOTES

This text was originally conceived of as a live performance. Should you be interested in performing it (or curious about the mechanics of the live performance), the following notes are for you.

You'll have seen, reading through this book, that there are two types of text: the main text and the stories. The stories, of which there are twelve, are denoted by their titles in the margin, a slightly smaller font and margin indentation on either side. Everything else is the main text.

The audience will always hear the main text, but in any given performance they will only hear six of the twelve stories.

To establish which stories are heard and which ones are not, at three points during the show, the performer asks the audience to choose from a selection of postcards that have the story titles written on them, and read them out loud.

The titles of the stories are:

1. Oyster
2. Fist
3. Bus
4. Hospital
5. Inbox
6. Book
7. Eggs
8. Teeth
9. Plane
10. Dog
11. Diner
12. Crabapple

Only hearing six of the stories results in a show that runs about seventy minutes. This form reinforces one of show's themes: the unknowability of a human life. And practically, it raises some challenges for the performer and creative team.

In these notes, I'll take you through the mechanics of the audience's involvement and the story selections. To that, I'll describe the set and props that were instrumental in our first production, and offer some suggestions, should you be staging this text. Then I'll detail how and when we got the audience to choose the stories, how we skipped over the untold stories, and what text we used to bridge the gaps.

I'll also touch on some of the physical and auditory elements only relevant to the live performance of this text.

Set and Props

Should you be staging this show, the only crucial design element is that you visually convey that there are twelve stories and, over the course of the show, make clear that the audience will only hear six.

You can borrow from what we did or create your own visual language to suit your venue.

Our set was comprised of a tall lifeguard chair in centrestage. The chair was distressed and attached to the side of the chair was a metal cup holder, a metal cup filled with water, a pencil holder and a charcoal pencil.

On the floor, in a circle around the chair, much like a clock face, there were twelve concrete plant pots, resembling urns. Each pot contained a tall stick, wrapped with (good-quality, fake) flowers and filled with sand. At the top of every stick there was a postcard, each labelled with the name of a story and affixed to the stick with a magnet. The postcards were arranged in order, beginning with *Oyster* at the 12 o'clock position and ending with *Crabapple* at the 11 o'clock spot.

It's essential that the audience be able to see all the postcards and sticks from the moment they sit in their seats through to the end of the show. For this reason, our sticks downstage were shorter than those upstage.

How and When Stories Are Selected

At three points throughout the performance, the performer gets the audience to choose which stories they'll hear.

To do this, I'd remove the appropriate postcards from their sticks and present them to the audience, fanned out.

The first selection is made from the first four stories (*Oyster*, *Fist*, *Bus* and *Hospital*). The second is made from the next five (*Inbox*, *Book*, *Eggs*, *Teeth* and *Plane*). And the third selection is made from the final three (*Dog*, *Diner* and *Crabapple*).

The first selection happens on page 7 after the line: *You'll choose the first two now*

While saying this, the performer will approach the audience with the first four stories (*Oyster*, *Fist*, *Bus* and *Hospital*).

The performer gets an audience member to choose a postcard. To prompt them to read it out loud, the performer says, *And you'll read it out loud*. Once they do, the performer repeats the audience's selection loudly and clearly, before getting another audience member to make the next selection.

Once two stories have been chosen, the performer replaces the postcards on their respective sticks, saying:

> So you will hear [first story selected]
> And you will hear [second story selected]

Then using the charcoal pencil, she crosses out the titles of the titles of the unselected stories, saying:

> You won't hear [first unselected story]
> And you won't hear [second unselected story]

And then the performer will say, *Good. That's decided.*

This ritual occurs for the second time on page 28 after the lines: *And you'll get it, anew: / Even your closest confidante / Will only ever know a handful of truths about you.* This time two audience members will choose two stories from the middle five stories (*Inbox*, *Book*, *Eggs*, *Teeth* and *Plane*). This time, while replacing the postcards on their respective sticks, the performer reiterates which two stories will be heard and which three won't.

The ritual occurs a final time on page 54 after the lines: *You didn't / You don't know why / You are getting better though / At accepting what you know / And what you won't.* This time two audience members will choose two stories from the final three stories (*Dog*, *Diner* and *Crabapple*). This time, the performer reiterates which two stories will be heard and which one won't.

The tone for these selections is warm without being saccharine, and ritualistic without being sanctimonious. It may take some practice to get it. You'll get it.

What Happens When a Story Is Selected?

Very important: The audience's selections *only* determine *what* stories are told. They do not affect the *order* in which the stories are told. That is to say, even if, in your first round of audience selections, *Hospital* is chosen first and *Fist* second, the performer will move through the text as written: they'll skip over *Oyster*, tell *Fist*, skip *Bus* and then tell *Hospital*.

When I got to a story that had been selected, I'd pluck the postcard off the stick, hold the postcard while I told the story, and then put the postcard on the ledge of the lifeguard chair when I was done telling it.

What Happens When a Story Is *Not* Selected?

When I reached *a story that hadn't been selected*, I'd hold the stick and the postcard while saying the replacement text, then pull the stick out of the pot and let it drop to the floor.

The untold story is replaced by a few lines to bridge the gap. The replacements for each story are as follows:

If *Oyster* is not selected by the audience, rather than tell the story, it's replaced with the following text:

> You'll meet a stranger
> You'll join her on an odyssey to the suburbs
> And it's—
>
> *Drop stick and postcard. A beat.*
>
> Anyway
> And before long, she'll be your best friend

If *Fist* is not selected, it's replaced with:

You stay with a childhood friend—nemesis,
someone who's always been a little bit prettier,
a little bit faster and exponentially more
organised than you
And you'll meet your dad there
And you'll find out you're more alike than you
thought—

Drop stick and postcard. A beat.

Anyway

If *Bus* is not selected, it's replaced with:

Drop stick and postcard. A beat.

Anyway

If *Hospital* is not selected, it's replaced with:

Make an attempt on her life
You'll visit her in hospital—

Drop stick and postcard. A beat.

Anyway
When you leave, you'll think, We both
committed to living lives that defied
convention. She nearly ended it and I'm
nowhere close.

If *Inbox* is not selected, it's replaced with:

From two friends close to death
One fighting it, the other running towards it
Your old best friend has made another attempt
on her life
And your childhood nemesis, the one you stayed

with on your first trip abroad all those years ago,
prettier, faster, more accomplished—is fighting
cancer—

Drop stick and postcard. A beat.

Anyway

If *Book* is not selected, it's replaced with:

And at the launch, he'll tell you something
about his childhood you wish you'd known for
twenty years—

Drop stick and postcard. A beat.

Anyway

If *Eggs* is not selected, it's replaced with:

The experience marks you—

Drop stick and postcard. A beat.

Anyway
And after five rounds, and some kitchen-floor
sobbing

If *Teeth* is not selected, it's replaced with:

You'll meet for a drink, and—

Drop stick and postcard. A beat.

Anyway
Afterwards you'll think, Why did I prize him so
high?

If *Plane* is not selected, it's replaced with:

Sitting beside a soldier—

Drop stick and postcard. A beat.

Anyway
A comment about young troops calling out for
their moms stays with you

If *Dog* is not selected, it's replaced with:

And finally, you get one
A puppy

But before he's fully grown, he's gone—hit by a
car—

Drop stick and postcard. A beat.

Anyway

If *Diner* is not selected, it's replaced with:

It's your old best friend—the one you met in the
dog park in your twenties
You haven't had contact in thirty-one years
You'll share a meal in a diner—

Drop stick and postcard. A beat.

Anyway
After

If *Crabapple* is not selected, it's replaced with:

His final act will be to plant a crabapple tree in
your back garden—

Drop stick and postcard. A beat.

Anyway

Dinging the Bell

Throughout the text there are lists of ways in which the body changes over time, for example:

> *You will have passed peak muscle mass*
> *You will produce less melatonin*
> *Your collagen production will be on the decline*

There are lots of these throughout the entire text. These anatomical changes are also indented on the page so you can clearly identify them. In performance, at the end of each of these lines, the performer dings/taps the cup of water with the charcoal pencil.

On page 42 where there is a long list of all the things you spend money on trying to stay young, each item on the list receives a ding after it's spoken. Throughout the list though, the dings build in pace until they're coming faster than the words and end in a frenzy, much like the scramble to hold onto youth, before thinking, Oh, who gives a hoot?

Staging

The movement and blocking were kept to a minimum in our first production. Generally, I was on the chair for the main text and on the floor to tell the stories.

At the end of the show, when I'd say, *You are spoken about in the past tense...* (page 74), I'd come down from the chair and slowly collect the discarded postcards with the titles of the untold stories written on them while I spoke. When I got to the line, *And things only you knew will die along with you* (page 75), I'd lay the postcards in my hands down on the floor. Then in silence, I'd pick up one of the flowerpots filled with sand and pour the sand over the untold stories.

Physical Repetitions

There are several refrains which appear throughout the text. I was interested in coming up with small, naturalistic gestures that I'd repeat with each refrain. For example, one of the refrains is:

> *You'll resolve to drink more water, eat more*
> *vegetables and exercise more*
> *And you will*
> *For a while*

I also had gestures for *You will work. Hard.* And *You'll ask your brother and god.* I didn't have gestures for the *Anyways* in the replacement text or for *Age is a feeling*—it felt important that those always be different.

The Song

The fragment of the song mentioned on pages 18, 48 and 74 sounds like this:

In performance it's hummed three times following the lines:

> *You'll do nearly everything alone, and hear yourself*
> *humming a few lines of a song your mother sang*
> *when you couldn't sleep* (page 18)

> *Months after her funeral you'll hum it* (page 48)

> *From the next room, you'll hear her hum it—those*
> *lines from the song your mother sang* (page 74)

The performer must hum it in a key that feels good for their voice. It doesn't have to sound pretty, just like something you've known forever.

Sound Design

After trying it both ways, the first production was performed without a microphone. Should we move to a larger venue, though, I'll likely use one as vocal control, the ability to use the full range of my voice and creating intimacy are the priorities.

Besides the fragment of the song hummed, there was no sound design or underscoring used in our first production. We felt it was important to let the text and the audience's imagination do the heavy lifting.

There are a few moments when the performer sings:

On pages 16 and 61, when you get to *Mama's planting trees*, etc. Those are all sung to the tune of 'Rose's Turn' from the Styne/Sondheim/Laurents musical *Gypsy*.

On page 72 when you get to *But it's mostly just the same note*,

I'd suggest singing it! All on the same note, until you get to 'note' and make it a different note.

A Word About 'God'

Raised without religion and deeply agnostic myself, the word 'god' once made me wince; however, I now consider it synonymous with some vague thing, bigger than myself, out there in the cosmos. If saying 'god' makes you feel uncomfortable for whatever reason, feel free to change all the mentions of 'your brother and god' in the text to 'your brother and the universe'.

ACKNOWLEDGEMENTS

Creating a play is like raising a barn—thanks to all who lent me a hand:

The theatres, organisations and their tireless staffs: Soho Theatre, especially David Luff and Maddie Wilson; Camden People's Theatre and AD Brian Logan; Summerhall, especially Verity Leigh and Tom Forster; The Rosemary Branch and AD Laura Killeen; and Soulpepper Theatre.

The creative team who brought it to life: Rose Hockaday, Zoë Hurwitz and Dan Carter-Brennan. Zoe Robinson was a big help early in the process. As was the incomparable wise-beyond-her-years Eliza Cass.

My director and dramaturg, Adam Brace—a terrific collaborator—who leapt in and worked assiduously with unparalleled attention to detail, sense of humour and intelligence. Thank you for championing this piece and helping me become a better writer.

The wonderful people who turned my words into a book: extraordinary and sensitive editor Matt Applewhite and Nick Hern Books; illustrator Jason Logan (dreams come true); my superb literary agent Kirsty McLachlan; Robert Moutrey, my love, who notated the piece of music I invented (and who's also seen every iteration, lugged around my props and set pieces and engaged in a continual conversation about the content of the show and how best to work).

The generous people who aided me with my research and development, in particular: Martina Steiger, Charlene Diehl, Taylor Trowbridge, Jasmine Chen, Talia Chai and Sarah McVie. Kathryn Mannix's book *With the End in Mind* was an incredible touchstone, as were my trips to Nunhead Cemetery. The *Plane* story features some text which is more or less lifted from a Reddit thread in which soldiers discussed their relationship with death. I'm so grateful to be privy to the insight. Much of the text about how age is felt in the body, regrets, advice and ways we spend money trying to stay young are inspired by members of my social-media community, who answered my prompts; your candour shaped the show.

Every audience member who attended a work-in-progress performance—your reactions are my favourite feedback.

Finally, my family, especially my parents, who, in their seventies, are still seizing life.

About the Illustrator

Jason Logan is the author of *Make Ink* and the founder of the Toronto Ink Company. His illustration work has appeared in *The New Yorker* and *The New York Times*.

www.jasonslogan.com

www.nickhernbooks.co.uk

facebook.com/nickhernbooks

twitter.com/nickhernbooks